Enchanted Mountain Whispers

B.G. Wetherby

Bloomington, IN   authorHOUSE®   Milton Keynes, UK

AuthorHouse™
1663 Liberty Drive, Suite 200
Bloomington, IN 47403
www.authorhouse.com
Phone: 1-800-839-8640

AuthorHouse™ UK Ltd.
500 Avebury Boulevard
Central Milton Keynes, MK9 2BE
www.authorhouse.co.uk
Phone: 08001974150

First published by AuthorHouse 4/27/2007

ISBN: 978-1-4343-0806-1 (sc)
ISBN: 978-1-4343-0805-4 (hc)

Printed in the United States of America
Bloomington, Indiana

This book is printed on acid-free paper.

Library of Congress Control Number: 2007902745

THIS BOOK IS DEDICATED
TO GOD.
WITHOUT HIM, I AM NOTHING.
<u>SPECIAL THANKS TO:</u>

MY WIFE DANI,
my inspiration and loving soulmate.

MY PARENTS....

OUR 8 CHILDREN:
Sare
Alisha
Austin
Tess
Markay
Brad
Steve
Jerry

Our 13 Grandchildren....

Thank you all for your support.

Enchanted Mountain Poems is not your typical "roses are red" poetry but, rather a powerful food for you to nurture upon. Many of us are starving for encouragement and direction in this perplexed era in which we live.

Our goal is to provide you with a

BIG, FAT, JUICY CHEESEBURGER IN A WORLD OF TOFU.

bon appetit

Contents

Life Poems

THE LAST SENIOR CITIZEN

Each time a senior citizen dies,
It's just not another human being,
But, a valuable pair of eyes are lost,
To all which they have seen.

The many changes in the lifestyles,
Stories of how it used to be.
Their wise advice is going silent,
Along with ethics and morality.

One at a time they're leaving us,
So are values and integrity.
Life is much more complicated,
Then the way used to be.

The elders knew what they were saying.
Their words were kept at any cost.
Most marriages worked and survived,
Another thing that we have lost.

Pride was taken in their jobs,
And it was done with care.
They prayed and ate together.
Those yesteryear's are no longer there.

The very last fiber is about to snap.
Which holds our family ties.
Who will tell us of how life used to be
When the last senior citizen dies?

THE RAINBOWS END

The storm is ending, the sun's peeking out,
Your life will change without a doubt.
Beautiful rainbows will be everywhere,
Plenty of smiles, you'll find them there.

You've passed through so much rain,
And you have endured so much pain.
You will heal, and you shall mend
As you draw nearer to the rainbow's end.

At the rainbows end you will find
Love, acceptance, and peace of mind.
Life can be so simple there,
Worry free and without a care.

Something's waiting on the other side.
Stay on the rainbow and enjoy the ride.
It won't be gold on the other end.
You just might find a rainbow friend.

Your dream's will be culminating soon,
You will sing a new and happy tune.
So if you feel your life descend.
You're getting closer to the rainbow's end.

INNOCENCE LOST

A boy up on the roof top,
With a scoped rifle in his hand.
High atop the local school,
Staring out across the land.

A teen girl, she's now pregnant,
Because she was running wild.
Frightened and confused,
She's now a child-bearing child.

A young boy robs a local store
To afford a drug to snort,
Dropping out of school,
Now he stands in court.

One kid calls in a bomb scare,
One kid chooses suicide,
One kid steals a car
And takes it for a ride.

At a party all were drinking
One decides to drive.
Giving friends a quick ride home,
None of them survived.

It looks like things are really good.
Yes, it's going rather well.
Parents, your neglected children are attending
My dress rehearsal known as HELL!

SATAN

Where Am I?

Often people lose themselves,
Then wonder how they lost their way.
Self worth hiding from them,
Eluding each and every day.

If you're around an alcoholic,
You will learn to drink.
If you're around a selfish person,
Selfish thoughts you learn to think.

Be with an abuser,
Someday you will abuse.
Be around a user,
Then, you learn to use.

If you're around a swearer,
Soon you learn to swear.
If they share their bodies with others,
Then you learn to share.

If they do not follow God,
Then you will learn to stray.
If they play their games with you,
Soon you team to play.

Be with someone who tears you down,
Well, then you learn to tear.
Be around little compassion,
Then you'll no longer care.

The wrong people make you self-destruct.
You'll end up with a lost identity.
Someday you'll ask the question,
Where did I lose me?

MISTAKES

The only thing in life that's easy
Are the mistakes that we tend to make,
The potential it is always there,
No matter what we undertake.

Apply the wisdom that you possess
Right from the start.
If you seek a proper answer,
Align your thoughts up with your heart.

DREAMS

Today I had a vision,
Just as plain as it could be.
Of what tomorrow might have in store,
In this life for me.

It may be a long time coming,
But, most good things usually do.
If you can wait upon your dreams,
They just may turn out true.

Sometimes they appear so close,
Sometimes, oh so far.
Never give up on your dreams,
No matter what they are.

ANGELS THERE

When faced with insurmountable odds,
When overcome by fear,
When exhausted and really needing help,
There's always someone near.

Overseeing and protecting,
Keeping a relentless watch on you,
With a gentle grasp upon your hand,
They will pull you through.

In any given circumstance,
Pain, concern, or care,
You will never go through it alone,
For there's always Angels there.

No Comparison

When you compare what you lack,
To what others now possess.
Confidence loses to intimidation,
Failure gives way to success.
Self worth becomes victimized,
Doubt dances with decisiveness.
Pessimism and panic become contagious,
And life becomes meaningless.

WHEN RACISM FALLS

A tree, is but a tree,
With a uniqueness of its own.
Much more noticed in a group,
than when it stands alone.

Each leaf clings with their own likeness,
But serves a purpose as do all.
In proper season all come together,
To make the colors of the fall.

God made us very similar,
Different races like the tree.
Real beauty lies within us too,
Where others seldom see.

If we bring our colors together,
Sharing the beauty that is within.
Racism will surely fall that day,
And the worlds autumn shall begin.

HOUR GLASS

In the hourglass
The moments pass,
Sifting grain by grain.
Simple specks of sand,
Life at hand,
For loss and not for gain.

With this day
An enormous price you pay,
Once gone, it's for eternity.
The sand that you possess
Now grows less and less,
So don't spend it foolishly.

OUR PAIN

No two snowflakes are similar,
All are different by design.
The only common denominator is,
All melt away with time.

Each one of us is different,
No two are the same.
With one exception to the rule,
Our common ground is pain.

Happiness and joy may vary,
Just like the depth of snow.
Our emotions are very season like,
They come-They go.

Inside all of us we carry pain,
God made us all this way.
An emotion that we carried forth
Into each new day.

Pain, the great pretender,
Masking what others might have done.
Some inflicted by our own doing.
A past, or present one.

With time, old pain may loosen
And slowly fade away.
Making room for all the new,
That we may receive today.

Not even Christ was free of it,
He knew anguish and knew pain.
God allows us to be Christ like,
So we all know the same.

As you interact with one another,
Focus beyond their fleshy skin.
Just as you, so they do too,
Have pain buried deep within.

THE AFFLICTED

Affliction, not pain, upon the innocent,
Is far greater of the two perils.
For, a loving heart that seeks new paths of healing,
Will eventually find a softness, in their pillow.
However, the afflicters never stray far from their
Troublesome road, and finds their walk as course,
As the place where they lay their heads to rest.

PROPER FOCUS

You will never risk anything
If you don't focus right.
Never reaching the best places,
With misdirection in your sight.

Do not focus on resistance
But rather the purpose of your plan.
Ask yourself the question, HOW?
Instead of the question, CAN?

When focusing on an objective,
The obstacles begin to disappear.
Your faith is but a shadow,
When eclipsed by fear!

HEARTACHE

Love is but a journey,
Where you'll find joy or pain.
You can be warmed by it's fire,
Or burnt by it's flame.
If love has been unkind to you,
And has left you with a burn,
What was destroyed,
God will replace,
So wait for it's return.

LIVE TODAY

When you're born, you begin to die.
When you die, you begin to live.
While existing in this world,
Give the best that you can give.
Some of us leave unexpectedly
And leave the rest in sorrow.
Be kind and loving to all around,
For they may be gone tomorrow.

Love Poems

LOVE OF A LIFETIME

Oh my heart is full of you today,
With warm, constant thoughts that won't go away,
I am so in love what can I say,
For I've found a special love in you.

There's a spring found in my every step,
You have kissed away the tears I've wept,
Locked inside of my mind and securely kept,
Is every precious moment spent with you.

I thought that I have known love before,
So many times, but I'm not keeping score,
You keep me craving more and more,
Oh, how I'm sweetly addicted to you.

I have never known a feeling like this,
My heart melts away with every kiss,
I lay awake each night for I don't want to miss,
Not even one thought of you.

I knew if I was patient that I would finally win,
Friends say that I support this silly little grin,
I am so thankful that fate let you in,
For I am so in love with you.

My view of life is different now,
I got through the past, but I don't how,
I have more happiness than the lord should allow,
Because I have been blessed with you.

They say that we all want a love of a lifetime,
And I'm so glad that you are mine,
Just throw away my past,
God saved the best for last,
In you I've found my love of a lifetime.

SO IT SEEMS

Calmness rises with your smile,
Your laughter brings tranquility.
There's peace within the words you speak,
Your heart brings serenity.
I have never met anyone like you,
Except maybe in a dream,
I'm on the road to happiness,
So it seems.

As I learn more about you
I question, how can it be?
You're everything that I've searched for,
Feel the chill inside of me!
Trapped for so long in darkened corners,
My hearts now lets out the screams.
You are the air that I need to breathe,
So it seems.

With the slightest thought of you,
My heart starts beating fast.
The life that I lived was not life at all,
As I reflect upon my past
Yes, I have missed everything,
But now the future gleams.
Life, until now was a waste of time,
So it seems.

It seems that I have started
To fall in love with you.
As I make the journey down the path,
I hope that you are coming too.
Don't anybody catch me,
For I've begun to fall
Into this long awaited prayer
That God answered after all.

TIME CAPSULE

Today is just a day
Father time shall sweep away,
Gone for all eternity.

But what will carry through
Will be my undying love for you,
Kept in a capsule deep inside of me.

TURMOIL

We do not have the rhythm,
Even though we hear the beat
When we try to dance,
We can not move our feet

Yet, the song goes on,
But we just stand and stare.
No words are ever spoken,
Are we being fair?

When we try to speak,
The other cannot hear.
We both are so distant,
Even though we're near.

We have a little spark,
But the fire just won't burn.
Possibly, we are not meant to be,
Maybe, it's not our turn.

Will the future let us know,
If we blew our chance?
Should we both turn and walk,
Or, should we stay and dance?

Nothing Short

God and time
Has made our love shine.
We area a fortunate two.

The days pass sweetly by.
Always, not but one day shy
Shall I fall short of loving you.

Easy Thing To Do

Sometimes I just can not believe
The feelings inside of me.
Loving you is simple,
Done quite easily.

You make every breath I take,
Such an easy thing to do.
I thank God each and everyday,
For blessing me with you.

Second Chance

In our lives we both have danced,
Each on different floors.
Both of us have learned to swim,
But, at different shores.
Oh, how the tide and music
Can change so suddenly.
How once sweet notes can soar,
How storms rock a once calm sea.
Through it all we've found one another,
It's our turn for romance.
I'll try and keep our water smooth,
And rhythm in our dance.

DREAMS SPAWN REALITIES

Is there a silver lining
In the clouds up above?
Will the answer comes by searching
Or waiting for love?
For now it is just a dream
On who will make my life complete.
My dream will spawn the reality
When we finally meet.

I would rather live life empty
Than settle for anything less.
Than what real love will bring to share,
And deserving happiness.
It doesn't matter if you are a millionaire,
Or push a cleaner's broom.
Inside this patient, waiting heart
You will have a room.

I would rather keep on dreaming
About my long awaited friend
Than accept mere infatuation
Where people hurt in the end.
It won't matter if you're a movie star
Or in the welfare line.
If you know how to love Agape,
You'll get this heart of mine.

With a wandering eye,
Along with constant prayer,
I believe that you do exist
And that you're out there.
Dreaming doesn't cost a dime,
It will only cost you time,
As I await the day that you come my way
When the dream spawns reality.

DON'T MAKE ME PAY

I know that you have been hurt before
And you want to take things slow.
I'll be patient, for I understand.
But there's something that you should know.

It was not me who brought you down
And caused your world to end.
The role that I now play will be okay,
I will start out as a friend.

Just don't make me pay
For what others did yesterday.
I'm not the one who caused you needless pain.
I'll kiss the tears from your eyes.
I'm not like the other guys.
Give me a chance for real romance,
Just don't make me pay.

Broken love has left your head spinning,
With fear along with doubt.
Take down the wall around you.
Please don't fence me out.

I just need this chance to show you
Love and security.
Don't be afraid, I know the price you've paid.
Just give this chance to me.

"I promise I won't hurt you."
That's probably something you once heard.
Anything said without an action
Is merely just a word.

One day at a time I will show you,
Your crystal heart is safe with me.
I won't let you down, I'll be around.
Take a chance and you will see.

LIKE I LOVE YOU

Oh, empty woman
In search of desire,
Have I replaced cold the empty nights
With passion and with fire?
Do I fill up
The void that you once felt
With soft, passionate kisses
That makes your body melt?

Am I all the wishing wells
Or the awaited fairy tale?
Am I every shooting star?
Or the wind upon your sail?
Am I restitution
For the prices that you've paid?
Am I every wish and prayer
That you have ever made?

Baby, am I worth
Every tear that you once cried?
Have I suddenly fulfilled
A life you've been denied?
Have I swept you off your feet?
Do I make your life complete?
Am I your dream come true?
Do you love me like, I love you?
Like I love you?

PHOTO LOVE

I am staring at your picture
That I have in front of me,
It is the only way to hold you now,
The way things have to be.

I'm lost within this picture.
Oh, you I truly miss!
Upon this precious photograph
I gently place a kiss.

I stroke my fingers through your hair
and rub your silken skin.
But this is just a photograph,
so now the tears begin.

Soon, I will hold you for real.
But an 8 x 10 is all I see.
This picture will have to do for now,
until you come home to me.

Someone Like You

Are you the awaited blessing,
That I've been praying for?
Countless nights perched by my bedside
My knees upon the floor.
Days spent questioning you existence.
At night, I prayed the doubts not true.
But, I've always known within my heart
There was someone like you.

So In Love With You

Once solely but a dream,
Backed up with constant prayer.
Then one day they both came together
When I saw you standing there.
Yes you are my vision,
To good to be true.
Thank God you're now reality,
For I am so in love with you.

SOMEDAY IT APPEARS

Life seems almost empty
In my hourglass of time.
I have so very much to give
To the one that I'll call mine.

Somehow love has forgotten me
Throughout these darker years.
When will I welcome its sweet light?
Someday, it appears.

Good things come to those that wait,
Many wise people say.
For now you are but the dream
That gets me through each day.

I wait with hope and patience,
While each new sunrise nears.
Eventually I know that you will come,
Someday, it appears.

GOING SLOW

New beginnings are often frightful,
When one's been hurt before.
Part of me just wants to run,
Another part to explore.

Some of me wants to open up,
Another to close up tight.
I can not afford one more mistake,
This time I must be right

I have this need forgoing slow,
Please be patient and understand.
Because I would rather build on rock,
Instead of shifting sand.

Brand New Start

Oh, the choices that I have made,
Emotional prices which I have paid.
Brokenness and life torn apart
Open season on a loving heart.

I have inventoried this heart of mine.
Still plenty of love, and beating fine.
An enormous amount that is left to give
With plenty of life that is left to live.

Bad love has made me very wise.
I'll see the wrong ones coming with these eyes.
Then I will just simply turn and flee.
They don't deserve what's inside of me

What I have left is reserved for you.
I know that God will lead you to.
This slightly bruised, but golden heart,
Fully mended for my brand new start.

LEARN TO FIX

I remember how you used to say
Those sweet three words my favorite way.
Softly whispered in my ear,
As you tightly held my body near.

My, how those words are now estranged
To these ears which have not changed.
The words you spoke, were they not true
When you said, "I love you?"

But if you do, then stay and fight,
For only one can't make it right.
Let's work together and as one,
So that we learn to fix and not to run.

Test Of Love

Love is not tested,
Until it's not returned.
Then, and only then,
Is the value learned.

Love remains unselfish,
Even in the sight of wrong.
For A heart that is given to the weak,
Will teach and make them strong.

LOVE CAN ALWAYS SEE

Beyond Faults,

Beyond Shortcomings,

Beyond The Moment,

And Beyond Ones' Horizon.

LOVE'S JOURNEY

Did fate bring you here?
Was it an answered prayer,
once whispered deep into the night?
Or, was it just plain luck?

No matter which journey united us,
Please know that with you in my life,
I continue to grow as a person, and that
My heart continues to grow with you...

SOMETIMES

Sometimes we give tenderness,
Sometimes pass out grief.
Sometimes we give loves pleasures,
Sometimes shake our heads disbelief.
Our lives are filled with sometimes
In all that we do.
But, one thing which is not a sometimes is,
Tomorrow I'll still be here for you.

TRANQUILITY

Long, moist and tender kisses,
A slow, smooth and gentle touch.
Your hugs, your smiles and your playfulness,
I miss these things, so much.

Falling to sleep nested in your arms,
You are my tranquility.
Life really isn't life at all,
When you're not here with me.

CHOOSING YOU

The search is finally over now.
Dreams and prayers, they have come true.
I found what I was looking for
on the day that I found you.

I tried to do it on my own.
Stormy waters I did find,
so I turned it over to the Lord.
I have found my peace of mind.

His magical hands, they calmed the sea
and sent me sailing straight to you.
Rainy days have all turned sunny.
Darkened skies have turned to blue.

What is in my past are simply shadows,
for the future is all I see.
I choose you for my remaining years,
just as you have chosen me.

Captivity

Day after day,
One constant thought.
Trapped in a daydream,
In which I am caught.
Oh, how I miss you,
Time slowly passes away.
Looking for blue skies,
Through this overcast gray.

My Everything

My every moment,
My every thought,
My every dream,
Which I have sought

My every pleasure,
That life could bring.
Fact is
You are my everything.

SOON

Soon, I will hold you in my arms.
Awaiting your passions, desires, charms.
I'm trying to get through one more day,
but time just slowly drags away.
It is so cold without your heat.
Soon, that will change when our lips meet.
My love, I truly miss you so,
more than you can begin to know.

Soon, the empty nights will disappear
when your sweet sighs, fill my ear,
Culminating in our special place,
Heart to heart, and face to face.
Each day I watch the setting sun
patiently waiting to be again as one.
I count the days two by two.
Soon, my love, I'll be with you.

SWEET SPARROW

Oh, sweet sparrow, how you once flew,
peacefully through skies so blue,
Breathing air which you've never known,
gracefully flying as you've never flown.

A free spirit carried you so high.
Oh, how you lived for that open sky.
Soaring to heights that you have never been,
determined to never land, nor descend.

Maneuvering freely without a care,
uninhibited soul, so full of flair.
Flamboyantly winging, full of grace,
well in command of your air and space.

Who caused you to swoop so low
crashing you to the ground below.
Where predators lurk in the grass and sage
to pounce on you with all their rage.

Escape, sweet sparrow, for you must soar
to those same heights where you were before.
Fly again Sparrow, like you once flew,
Peace and happiness will return to you.

GRATIFIED SOUL

I find a special comfort,
Like none that I have known.
Your love is very special,
My, how my heart has grown.
You bring tranquility with every touch,
Each kiss, and embrace.
My soul is completely gratified,
For all that you have replaced.

DIFFICULT TIMES

Where have all the sweet words gone?
Lately it seems that all is wrong.
Instead of smiles, we seem to cry.
Both wanting to quit, instead of try.

We must bandage up our cuts left deep.
Replace these tears with smiles to keep.
Forgive one another for damage done.
Making our hearts again beat as one.

These walls we have built, they must come down.
Find the smiles and lose the frowns.
God, will cleanse the resentments away.
If we only give it to Him today.

We must do this as a team
To fulfill our goals and live our dream.
Let's show each other that our love is true.
I'll make the effort, how about you?

Culminated Quest

Hand in hand, we step in time.
Poetry with the perfect rhyme.
A moonlit beach beneath the stars above.
The moment's right, we feel the love.

The tides roll gently upon the shore.
Sweet addiction desires soar.
Your touch gently sweeps my face.
Our bodies lock in a deep embrace.

My lips seek yours and the moisture there.
The wind blows freely through your hair.
Our breathing begins to intensify.
A moan, a scream, a gentle sigh.

The ocean whispers, a distinctive sound.
Bodies pressed together upon the ground.
Moving perfectly with each new wave.
Moments of pleasure, forever saved.

Crying our names out to the moon
Our pounding hearts are finely tuned,
We have now culminated our quest.
Now it's time for peaceful rest.

JUST ONE PRAYER

In the silence of my room,
Which now seems to be my tomb,
I think of the yesterdays gone by.
I still see your face
every moment, every place.
My strength drained, I start to cry.

Out of the window I now stare,
Just wishing you were there
as you were not that long ago.
I sure do miss your touch
so very, very much.
There's no way that I can let you know.

My lonely lips do miss
the way we used to kiss.
Why, oh why did you have to go?
How can I make you see
that we were meant to be?
I love you more than you shall ever know.

So much hurt down deep inside,
Hurt I surely cannot hide,
In plain sight for all the world to see.
If God would grant me but one prayer,
For it all seems so unfair,
I'd ask Him to bring you back to me.

Heartbeat

No one has ever treated me,
In such a very special way.
The smiles that I wore in my past,
Are worn quite differently today.
I am thrilled, and overfilled,
My life is now complete.
The world hears a gentle spirit play,
When they hear my heartbeat.

BEAUTIFUL CREATIONS

I've seen so many wondrous things
Sculptured from God's own hand.
Mountains, canyons and the lakes,
a great desert of white sand.
The splendor of His sunsets,
Stars streaking across the skies.
God surrounded us with awesome beauty,
to bring pleasure to our eyes.

In six days all things created.
Resting on the seventh one.
All for our own benefit,
What a glorious job He's done,
If I only had one choice to make,
Of His most beautiful creation true,
The choice would be so simple,
For my answer would be you!

THE GHOST OF YOU

As I sit within this empty house,
so bare since you've been gone,
I try to figure out some things,
Like, where did we go wrong?

To this day I can not understand
how this all came about.
The ghost of you still haunts this place
since the day that you moved out.

I still see your face upon the pillow
as I turn out the light.
I still feel your body next to mine,
deep within the night.

Sometimes I even hear your voice,
I actually answer to your calls.
But again, it's just the ghost of you
that lingers within these walls.

I am fine when I'm outside this house,
for I'm gone throughout the day.
But at night, you still have me enchained
with this ghost that won't go away.

STRANGER IN A LOVELESS LAND

I'm looking for love, and I'm not faring well.
Maybe I'll find it, but only time will tell.
A loving heart is so tough to sell
Is anyone looking for a deal?
On a loving heart that's real?

I don't want money, nor do I want fame,
This heart is not a toy for a game.
Is there someone out there that feels the same?
Then I'm looking just for you,
For a loving heart that's true.

Love, Acceptance and Security.
Oh, what a great life that would be.
To be loved for simply being me.
Does anyone out there understand?
Or am I just a stranger in a loveless land?

I need someone who 'll love me exclusively,
The way that God meant it to be,
Who 'll spend their time loving, not changing me.
Will you be there tomorrow too?
Like I will be for you?

My arms are open to hold you tight.
To see me in love would be a sight.
Is there someone who'll take away the lonely night?
I'll give away this heart for free
To that someone who's meant for me.

Love, Acceptance and Security
.Oh, what a great life that would be.
To be loved for simply being me.
Does anyone out there understand?
Or am I just a stranger in a loveless land?

I know that you're out there somewhere, someplace.
Come and claim these sweet kisses for your face.
Take away this loneliness and leave no trace.
Staring into your eyes that gleam,
Or are you just a foolish dream?

DIFFERENCES

Who am I?
Who are you?
Lovers once, now distant strangers,
Lost, without a clue.
If we both seek resolution,
Change is where we start.
First, we look deep within.
To examine our own heart.

JUST HANGING ON

I know that things between us
at the present don't seem right.
What once sparked and once glistened
No longer looks as bright.

Everyone searches for excuses
and an easy out.
Instead of sweat for success,
we would rather pout.

It's a disposable generation.
Razors, diapers, swimsuits and pens.
Cameras, lighters and marriages,
Even a contact lens.

We think that the grass is greener
on the other side.
That is just problem relocation,
we would rather run and hide.

Society is selfish and so lazy.
Now there is no shame.
Instead of seeking solutions,
it's much easier to blame.

I don't want to be a failure;
I made a vow to you.
I hope that you truly feel the same.
As the way I do.

ABSENT TREASURE

Here I sit, miles away.
Yet my heart is next to yours today.
Beating as one, separated as two,
Inside of my heart are loving thoughts of you.

Space is but distance
that our bodies now be.
Inside of my heart,
you are held close to me.

Kept as a treasure,
so strong and secure,
where it shall remain
so loving and pure.

Locked deep in my heart,
your love's safe with me,
for you, my sweet love,
Hold the only key.

ANGEL OF THE LAKE

I walk along the waters edge
Accompanied by a lonely, empty frown.
Water rippling from my feet,
my head sadly hanging down.

Suddenly I felt God's gentle touch;
it's something one cannot mistake.
I lifted my head and turned it toward
the distant shore of this great lake.

There I saw an angel
extending out her waiting hand.
A radiant glow about her,
standing in the sand.

Was my prayer being answered?
Yes, my Lord does care.
But how do I get across the water
to the angel standing there?

"Your faith will make you strong," said God.
"Your search for love will see you through."
"I once moved the sea for Moses."
"I shall do the same for you."

Faith can move a mountain,
and build bridges across the sea.
Trust in Him as you should,
And believe in destiny.

MOON MAGIC

One cool spring night, beneath the moon,
we both danced to a romantic tune.
A deserted road in the still of the night,
under the stars it felt so right.

Our bodies pressed so tightly near,
without care, without fear.
Lips full of passion and hot desire,
and pounding hearts so full of fire.

I gently stroked your silkened face,
Embracing the moment of this perfect place.
Never encountering a night like this,
full of passion, full of bliss.

It happened on this magical night,
underneath that moon so bright.
You took my heart on a fantasy true.
On that night, I danced in love with you

CHANCE, FATE, OR GOD'S REWARD?

Oh, how sadness, and an ugly emptiness
has adorned my life,
wearing on me like a waterfall,
chiseling away on its solid rock base.

Heartache upon endless heartache,
swimming in this dark sea of disappointment.
Within its turbulent and destructive waters,
I am pulled beneath by the relentless currents.

How has happiness eluded me?
Why has love steered clear of my grasp?
Not just briefly, but for an entire existence.
Slipping through my hands as sand through an hourglass.

Out of fear, I ran from loves value,
Locking the windows and doors to my inner soul.
The past taught me to hide from the very source,
that I need to nurture upon.

Then suddenly an angel appeared before me.
Was it by chance, by fate, or God's reward?
With a touch of your hand you have cast my fear aside,
and have given me completeness of life everlasting.

Secret Seeds

You have planted a seed forever,
deep inside of me,
so deep that it must stay hidden
for no one else to see.

No light can ever reach it,
for it will surely grow.
A beautiful flower which must stay hidden,
for it is not allowed to show.

The seed is fully fertilized,
Buried deep within the ground,
for it can only blossom
when no one is around.

Some day it may bloom openly
for the entire world to see.
But for now this secret seed remains
Planted deep inside of me.

Elusive Dream

The beauty of a fresh new day,
Harnessed by bittersweet delight,
from quite an elusive dream
which I'm privileged with by night.

Overtaken by serenity
Upon arrival at this place,
I search amongst the silhouettes
Until I see your face.

My eyes feast upon your beauty,
then passions turn to hot desire.
We culminate our time away
until our bodies tire.
Morning arrives much too quickly,
Once again we must part.
Each time becomes more difficult,
for I'm a prisoner of my heart.

Disappearing right before my eyes,
as the dawn begins to gleam.
Do you exist in another's thoughts?
Are you someone else's dream?
So I pray my day away,
With hopes that you are real.
For I must free what's inside of me,
I must tell you how I feel.

You leave me with an anxious heart
Where you have burrowed deep,
I must have you throughout the day,
As I do when I'm asleep.

My Last Wish

One coin left inside my pocket,
I came upon a wishing well.
Hesitantly I tossed it in,
now only time will tell.

Whether my wish will be granted,
Or, I shall be denied.
Peace of mind or empty pockets,
At least I know I tried.

Once I had so many coins,
all were wasted in the past.
Broken dreams, and empty promises,
now I'm down to my last.

Life is but a coin toss,
Whether or not your dreams come true.
With my eyes closed, I heard the splash,
Then wished that I had you.

Ready To Fly

I was nursing my own wing
Which was damaged by a thorn.
When I came across a hurting angel
whose wings were slightly torn.

She had a special radiance
that would make a blind man see.
It brought a special brightness
to a world so dark to me.

When I gazed into her eyes,
I saw pain buried deep within.
To abuse such a giving, tender person.
Truly is a sin.

I realized there was an angel left
In a selfish world so filled with hate.
This angel who was knocked off course.
Satan's plan turned to holy fate.

I am strong again because of hope.
I now clearly stand upright.
I am not afraid to fly again,
now I'm ready to take flight.

I hope that I can help repair
the wings that other people tore.
So that I may fly with this angel,
and soar, and soar, and soar.

THE SPARK

Once solely but a dream,
So far from truth as truth could be.
An entertaining thought within my mind,
with no room for reality.

Expectations of what I sought,
with no chance you did exist.
Yet, the heart felt quite differently,
so the dreams persist.
From a dream you indeed appeared.
With one look I realized
the fictitious someone believed not true,
now stood before my eyes.

Overwhelmed by a blinding light
Cast from the cold and empty dark,
my hearts' fires now burns amuck,
a reaction to your spark.

TENDER HEART

Wandering through an aimless life,
I came across a tender heart
that made a great impression,
Right from the very start.

I could tell that she once glittered
in a better yesterday,
but invested in those not worthy,
now the years have quickly slipped away.

Shattered dreams and broken promises
Restarts that will not end.
Searching in a hardened world
for another tender-hearted friend.

A heart of gold, so full of love.
But it's buried deep within
where others could not see it,
for it fears to love again.

Skeptical now of all around,
less hopeful day by day.
Tired of chasing rainbows
falsely put within the way.

I know that path which you have traveled,
For I've made that journey, too
While searching for the tender heart
That I've finally found in you.

Keeper Of My Heart

Just a short time ago, I lived with an abundance
of inner emptiness.
Where my heart was once positioned
now stands a great black hole.

It took an enormous amount of strength
to pull together and reconstruct
the scattered fragments of a heart destroyed
from the yesterdays gone by.

You have pieced together the shattered crystals
of a heart that once was whole.
A treasure decimated by those of incompetence,
not worthy of holding something so priceless.

This crystal heart is whole again,
Full of love for you to sweetly nurture upon.
Although still fragile, I freely give it to you,
trusting that no harm shall come to it.

Openly I shall give you loyalty and dedication,
along with honor, trust, and deep respect.
Into thy gentle hands, I place this heart of crystal,
grateful for the emptiness that you have replaced.

You have engineered a task that seemed impossible.
You solely filled the once depleted.
You have reconstructed the once destroyed.
For this, you shall be the keeper of my heart.

PEACE UPON THE LAND

So many years of turmoil,
Lonely nights that knew no end
Awaiting the Lord's peaceful promise
Through this angel He would send.

One stormy sea into another,
Calm waters not within my sight,
Looking for a special love
Who'd calm my life and make it right.

Life has given me merely crumbs.
I need my slice of pie.
Searching for a tranquil life
and peace before I die.

One glorious day you just appeared,
Worthy of each tear which I have cried.
Mending all the brokenness,
you're what I have been denied.

One passionate kiss from your sweet lips,
One soft touch from your gentle hand,
One precious look into your eyes
Has restored peace upon the land.

MIDNIGHT PRAYER

I made a wish this winter,
Upon a star one night.
I made it to the brightest one,
The one that filled the sky with light.

I guess it wasn't just a wish,
But rather a pleading prayer.
For God to bring me a special love,
To a life that's been unfair.

That star really wasn't a star at all,
But God's gentle, caring ear,
Swooping down to listen
And drying each and every tear.

God will leave some prayers unanswered,
While some He will grant true.
That star-filled night He heard my words,
For He led me straight to you.

Sweet Time

We haven't known each other
for that very long.
I may not have all of the rights
for those who've done you wrong.

I want you comfortable and at ease,
So that your eyes can clearly see,
that love, not harm, exists in my heart.
I will accept what you give to me.

We will let the moments form between us,
and let sweet time just slip away,
Living second by second, minute by minute,
Hour by hour, and day by day.

Time's the greatest gift right now
that I can give to you.
Then you will see that it is not just today.
I will be here tomorrow, too.

Silent Journey

Each new day that I awaken
is but another that I greet.
I ask myself each new morning,
is it today that we meet?

I stare at every passerby,
asking myself, "are you the one?"
Hoping that our eyes ignite,
like the blazing sun.

I hear your heart, it's barely beating.
I'm honing in upon the sound.
I just know that I will find you soon.
Yes, you will be found.

Your heartbeat may be muffled
from hurt and resentment in your past.
Soon I'll stand before you,
To free your heart at last.

Conditional lovers say it's a fairy tale.
Skeptics say that it's not true.
Frightened hearts will keep their distance.
The misinformed don't know what to do.

I know that you are out there,
And that you shall rise above.
My ideal mate truly does exist,
so does this ideal love.

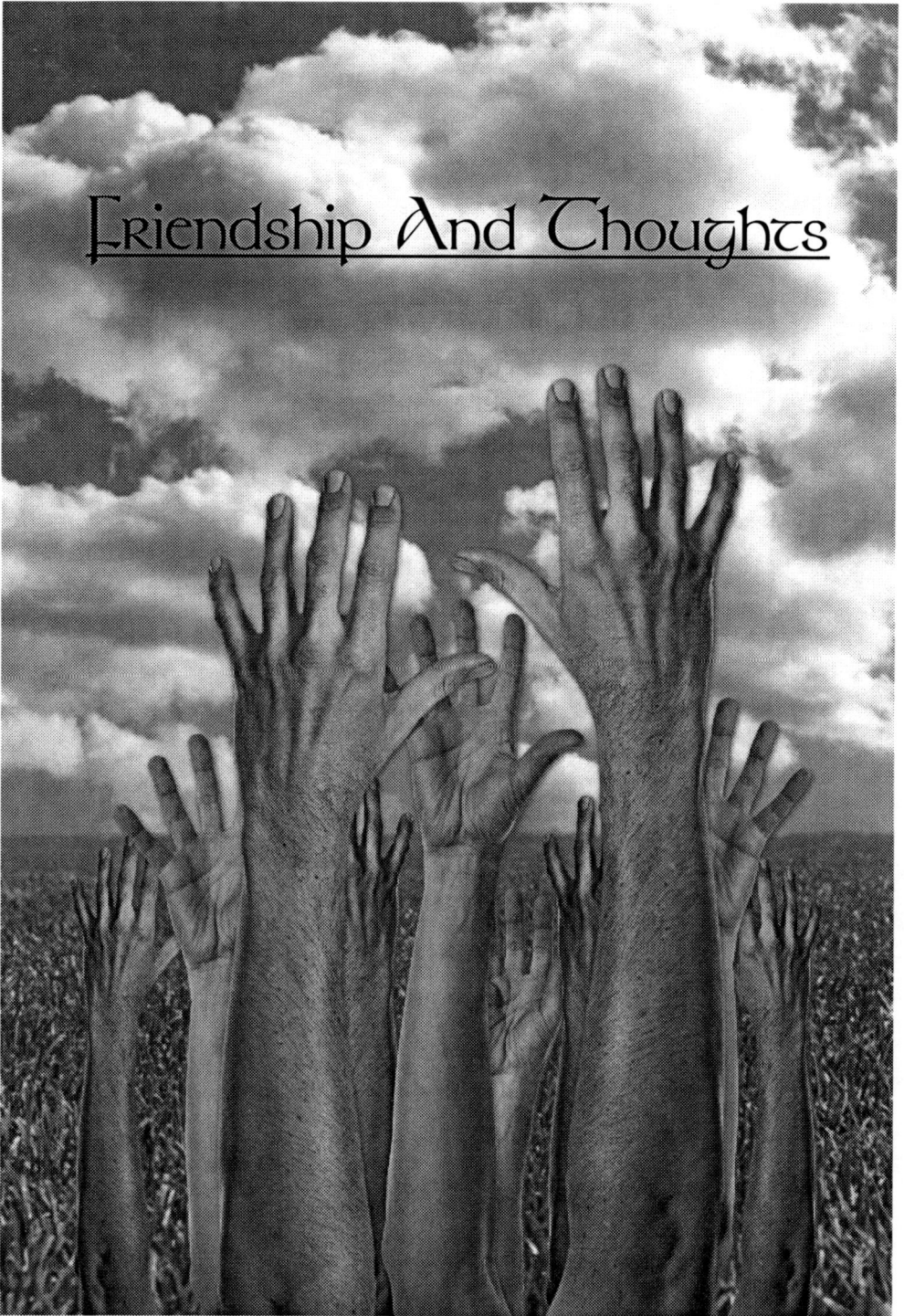

Friendship And Thoughts

GRATEFUL HEART

Like footprints in the sand,
Or tracks left upon the snow,
You leave a trail of gratitude
No matter where you go.

As an artist's brush touches canvas,
Like a note touches a singing Lark,
As the ocean touches distant sky,
Your friendship has left its mark.

PRAYER FOR A FRIEND

I sent a prayer to God today
Because you are my friend.
I asked for Him to bring your problems
Abruptly to an end.
I prayed for resolution,
And for all your trials to cease.
But most of all, oh friend of mine,
I asked for God to bring you peace.

PRAYER FOR YOU

If I wrote God a letter,
This message I would send,
I would ask Him to give you happiness,
And for your trials to reach an end.
We both know that's not reality,
So I sent it the only way,
In a very special prayer
That I said for you today.

My Friend

Whenever I could use a friend,
You are but a thought away.
If I need encouragement
You know just what to say.
When I need a shoulder,
You are always there.
I can surely count on you,
Anytime or anywhere.
So, today I say thank you
For being there until the end.
One of life's greatest joys,
is having you as a friend.

DAYDREAM

Entrenched in a prolonged daydream,
A repetition which I am caught
Such sweet intoxication,
Of my every thought
Held captive by serenity,
Inner peace long overdue.
Fortified in the core of my mind,
Are my thoughts of you.

TRUE FRIEND

A friend is a friend
And a true friend indeed.
Will be there to share the laughter
And in your greatest time of need.
They are right there in the thick of it
Should you take a fall.
But, if their heart and arms aren't open,
Then they are not a friend at all.

Friend Of Mine

Oh, friend of mine
So filled with care.
Whenever you are needed
You are always there.

To oversee and comfort me,
With all that I go through.
Life is much more simplified,
With a friend like you.

The Pouring Rain

Today, the rain dampens my heart.
A normal thing, while we are apart.
When you return, the sun shall too.
I am overpowered, with thoughts of you.

Sparkling Thoughts

Thoughts of you run peacefully,
Through my heart and mind.
Your friendship is a treasure,
That I was fortunate to find.

Sparkling like a priceless diamond,
With a glow that will not end.
You provide a special radiance,
My kind and thoughtful friend.

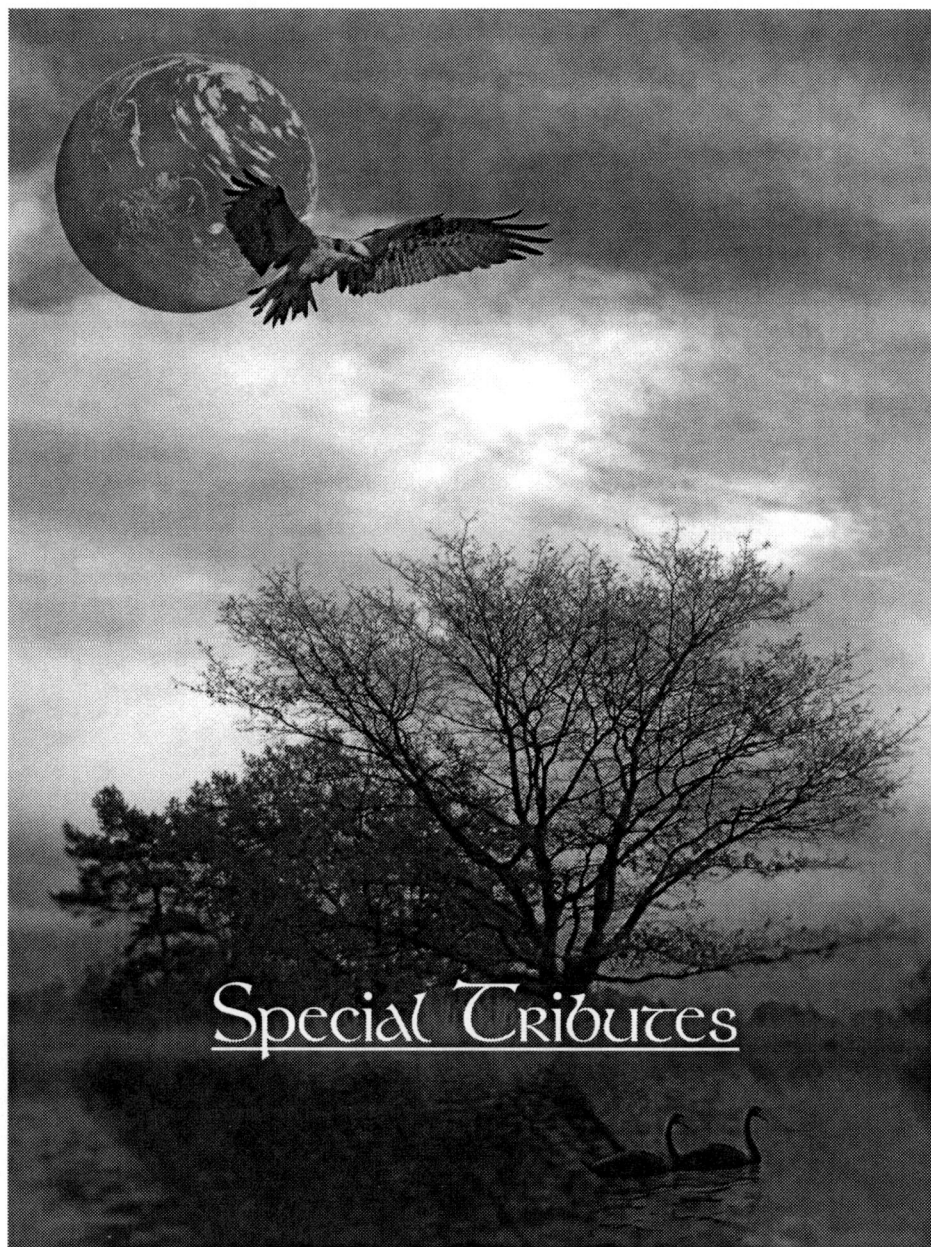

Special Tributes

ALWAYS THERE

When I needed nurturing,
Mother, you were there,
And if I needed punishing,
You were always fair.

When I lacked direction,
Mom, you lent a guiding hand.
If I had a problem,
You would always understand.

When I needed encouragement,
Mom, you knew just what to say.
When I needed structure,
You provided it each day.

When I think back to my childhood,
To the memories that I once knew.
I was extremely fortunate,
To have a Mom like you.

A MOTHERS LOVE

You've given so much of yourself
Throughout all these years.
Some days I made you smile,
Most days I caused you tears,
Now that I've grown, out on my own,
And life is clear to see.
As I reflect,
I've gained great respect,
For the mom that you've been to me.

SINGLE PARENT HOME

A single dad or a single mom.
As you know your life is seldom calm.
Well the job is real tough,
And the hours are so long.
You dig for strength just to carry on.

There are many roles that you must play.
New challenges await you everyday.
Yet you are only one person,
Yes that's true,
Even though you play the part of two.

Sacrifices, they must be made.
You do without so that the bills get paid.
Time goes by quickly,
As the children grow up fast
I refuse to make them pay for my past

So you put your life on hold.
You teach the kids and watch their lives unfold.
The rewards will truly payoff,
Just you wait and see. For soon you will have to set them free.

Another page it has been turned.
Through it all a lesson learned.
Real love is unselfish,
It requires sacrifice.
It comes back to you and it's worth the price.

FOR MY CHILDREN I WOULD DO ANYTHING,
AS I TRY TO BRING THEM UP ON MY OWN.
I MUST SHAPE A YOUNG WOMAN OR MAN.
THE BEST WAY THAT I CAN.
ALL ALONE.
THIS SINGLE PARENT HOME.
IN A HOUSE WHERE LOVE IS KNOWN.

Daddies Girl

The first time that I saw you,
I saw the very best part of me
As I turned my eyes unto the Lord
And thanked Him gratefully
For letting an angel slip away
And land here in my heart.
Oh, I've been blessed with you, my child,
Right from the very start.

It started when you learned to walk
And you took those steps all on your own.
Then came the first day of kindergarten,
My, how you have grown.
Quickly came your graduation,
Off to college you moved away.
Then I gave you to another man
On your wedding day.

So I sought out a quiet place
And raised my head up high.
I said, "Lord, this is very hard."
He saw this grown man cry.
"I've spent a lifetime of letting go of her
With every stage that she's gone through."
GOD said," I know that it's difficult,
I felt the same when I gave her to you."

How can this be,
The Lord doing this for me?
He's given me much more than I deserve.
You took control of my very soul
When you arrived upon this Earth.
You've been daddy's little girl since birth.
Thank you, Lord, for sharing her with me!

Mother Appreciation

WHEN I NEEDED TO SAY THANK YOU,
MOST TIMES I FORGOT.
THOUGH THE WORDS WENT UNSPOKEN,
YOUR ACTIONS MEANT ALOT.

IT APPEARED THAT I TOOK YOU FOR GRANTED
BUT MY HEART NEVER FELT THAT WAY.
SOMETIMES IN OUR BUSY LIVES,
WE NEGLECT JUST WHAT WE NEED TO SAY.

NO ONE APPRECIATES YOU MORE,
THAN THE WAY I DO.
THE WORDS SHOULD HAVE COME MORE OFTEN,
MOTHER, I LOVE YOU.....

THANKS DAD

I was a child, often wild,
Such unruliness I did bring.
I caused a strain, I was a pain,
And I knew everything.
Then at last, as the years flew past,
I put some focus in my sight
What you taught me, I now see,
Dad, you were right!

Fare Thee Well My Child

Time surrenders to no one.
So the years have quickly passed.
You've grown into a young adult,
Seemingly, much to fast
I remember holding you as a newborn,
Tucking you into bed at night
The nest is only confining you,
For you're ready to take flight

Some moments could have been better,
While others I'd never trade.
Circumstances often made it difficult,
In the role that I played.
But everything that you've accomplished,
Shall make you standout in a crowd.
Now as you go, always know,
That you've made me proud.

Fare thee well my child,
You have blossomed on this day.
Leaving your childhood days behind,
Wings now wisk you away.
As you fly, new open sky,
May you attain all you hope to find.
Fare thee well my child,
You will be on my mind.

HEALING HANDS

Concerned and frightened
Patients seek you out
For advice and hope,
To replace their doubt

For you give all comfort,
They trust your skills,
To heal their pain
and cure their ills.

Hours, often long
Dedicated, you are there
With understanding, with compassion
And quality of care.

Your words bring needed trust,
With all that you speak,
To everyone in need
Whenever they are weak.

Thank you so much Doctor
For all that time demands.
And for everything that you do
With your healing hands.

ANGELS OF CARE

(A Nurses Tribute)

Often thankless, you go about your duties,
Extreme hours very long.
On the brink of sheer exhaustion,
Still mentally you carry on.

Administrators, and sometimes doctors,
Add stress that you don't need.
Yet diligently you carry forth.
Such a rare and special breed.

You are always there, or close by
To ease our aches and pains.
Kindness overflows from your soothing heart,
Compassion fills your veins.

While we're at our weakest point,
Our burdens you shall bear.
God made you a special blessing,
As His Angels of care.

TEACHERS

I want to thank you, teacher
For the patience that you've shown me,
Especially when I can't focus on
What you want for me to see.

You never give up on a child,
Teaching all students bad or good,
And for not getting the recognition
Or the wages which you should.

Often caught up in the middle
Without support from parents or the school,
Educating is your sole concern,
Using every possible tool

You have an enormous impact
On our lives in the years ahead,
So I thank you now, ahead of time
While it can be said.

THE EAGLE FLIES

Yes, I am an American,
I will not run from fear.
I will not forget the founding fathers,
Nor the freedom which I hold dear.

Live free or die.
That is just our way.
Our hands are now joined as one,
Across the U.S.A.

The Eagle flies once again
To protect this great and noble land,
You will never see these colors run,
And united we shall stand.

Brothers and sisters that we have lost
Will not have died in vain.
Terrorist may have hurt our nest,
But the Eagle still remains!

New York Is Burning

(A Special Tribute To The New York Fire and Police Departments)

Shamelessly, we took you for granted
As you served us everyday.
Horror gave birth to realization
Of the respect that we should pay.

You put your lives on the line
Each time you answered an alarm,
As you go about your business,
Protecting us from harm.

Relentless in your bravery,
Never showing when afraid.
We will remember your heroism,
And the price that you paid.

911, a day of terror,
Which turned into Hell,
Buried beneath smoldering rubble,
As two mighty giants fell

Regrettably, cowards were the victors
On that gruesome September day.
Unforgettable memories of your valor
Within our hearts forever stay.

From this day forth the rest of you
Will receive the respect that you deserve.
May God Himself protect all of you,
As you protect and serve.

Number 3

Are legends made or are they born?
The greater the loss, the longer we mourn.
An end of an era, the start of a tale
Of a grand champion we knew as Dale.

His popularity put racing on top,
Then that once mighty engine came to a stop.
May the stories be many of his legacy
Which ended too quickly and tragically.

Numerous times Dale hit a wall
And walked away with no scratch at all
Yet this crash was minor comparably,
But it ended the reign of car number 3.

Time will not heal nor erase
The way that Black Bow Tie used to race,
Or, the championships and victories.
He left us with many memories.

Dale, we'll miss you on the track.
If only God would take that last lap back.
We feel your presence at every race,
As me drivers all battle for second place.

THE DEBT

Thank you for always being there,
For your compassion, love and care.
For being stern when you had to be.
For the values that you 've instilled in me.

For a mind to see just what is real,
For a loving heart that helps me feel.
For the years of patience that you've shown.
For the tools to live life on my own.

For making my childhood secure and nice,
For your unselfishness and sacrifice.
Mom, thank you on this special day,
For a debt that I can't repay.

TWIN BROTHERS

(September 11th, 2001)

Twin brothers once stood side by side
Now great catacombs for those who've died.
Americans, destroyed by terrors reign,
Filling all hearts with senseless pain.

Financial centers at their birth,
Grew tall and proud from the earth.
Arms of glass caressing the sky
At a better time with days gone bye.

Mighty towers that once stood tall,
Which spineless cowards caused to fall.
Once the steel and concrete hit the ground,
We used these twins to rally around.

We'll miss the twins that once stood firm,
Which terrorists used to make us squirm.
Twin brothers destroyed on our own land,
They may have fallen, but now we stand!

THOSE DAMN YANKS

In the house that Ruth built,
Constructed by his fame,
Lurk the ghosts and memories
From many heros of the game.
Baseballs greatest champions,
Gave birth to Murderers Row.
Gehrig, Ruth and Meusel
Gave way to Dimaggio.

Then came a kid from Oklahoma,
Mantle was his name.
Home runs were the Mick's forte,
Roger Maris was the same.
Scooter, Dickey, and Ali Reynolds,
McCarthy, Muggins, Houk and Case.
Gomez, Larsen, and Whitey Ford,
Yogi and Elston at home base.

Richardson, Kubek, Clete and Tresh,
Pepitone, Michaels, and the Moose.
Sparky, Mel and Righetti,
Chambliss, Catfish and the Goose.
Willie, Pags, White and Winfield,
Munson behind the plate.
Bucky, Rivers, Nettles and Reggie,
Octobers have been great.

Fear struck forth from many a hitter.
What could possibly be more frightening
Than having to stand, with bat in hand,

Against Louisiana Lightening?
Gone and back, gone and back Billy.
Sweet Lou, another famous curser.
Oh,the beauty which was in the swings
Of Mattingly and Murcer.

Distinguished careers along the way,
We wont forget the impacts made,
By Cone, Baylor, Kaat, Raines,
Pettit, Wells and Wade.
Ruben, Gooden, Luis Tiant,
The Rocket, and Darrel Strawberry,
The Niekro brothers, Rickey Henderson,
Tommy John and Jimmy Key

We will remember the sad goodbyes
To Tino, Scott and Paul.
All part of another era.
We'll sure miss you all.
New heros still remain with us,
A-Rod and Torre,
Jorge, Jason, Mussina, MO, Derek,
Godzilla and Bernie.

From the players of today,
And to all who've come and gone.
Gehrig to Derek, Bemie to Babe,
Yankee pride runs strong.
A new Century now has begun,
For the past we give our thanks.
We look forward to tomorrows' stars
Playing for those Damn Yanks.

Goodbye Teacher

(A Tribute to My Mother)

Mom, you taught us how to love
And to show compassion to all around.
Now you lie before us still,
In silence, without a sound.

You put the Bible in our hands,
As well as Jesus in our hearts.
We'll keep all that you've instilled in us,
For it is time for you to part.

Thank you, mother, for a job well done.
We promise it will not go for naught.
As we pass forward to our own children
Everything of which you taught.
Goodbye, we know that it's time to leave,
So enjoy your eternal rest.
Lord, watch over her, as she did with us,
For you have taken our very best.

THE PROMOTION

Sometimes I steal some quiet time
From my often busy day.
Where I can set my mind free,
Just to wander away.
Journeying to treasured places
Which are held endeared.
Back to when we shared a life,
Before you disappeared.

Thoughts of what you taught me,
Are now serving me so well.
The smiles that you wore each Christmas,
And the stories that you'd tell.
Our talks, and the moments shared,
As well as many other things
Before God reached down and took you,
And fitted you with wings.

Now you are an angel
Looking down from above.
I won't forget our time together,
Nor will I forget the love.
To this day I still shed tears,
Bitter sweetly they do flow.
I know that God promoted you,
But I still miss you so.

THE LOVE INSIDE OF YOU

The greatest product of a love so deep
Is something that you will always keep.
It shall never go away.
There to remind you every day.

Of a special love starting with two.
Now it's carried well inside of you.
Conceived in love months ago,
Deep within, the love still grows.

The birth of a child, such a wondrous thing,
what a special bonding that it will bring.
A newborn child, a newborn face,
Soon to take its rightful place.

Solely yours and here to stay.
Only God Himself can take it away.
The reality is, and it's true,
It is a world of love inside of you.

THE FALLEN

Our nation, it is free today
Thanks to the fallen who have died.
American blood bravely spilled,
American tears proudly cried.

Beginning with our founding fathers,
Who lost in order to gain.
With every battle after that,
American freedom was maintained.

To protect this great life that we have
And will never be denied.
The freedom that we enjoy today,
Is a blanket that others did provide.

We have paid dearly for it all,
Just to see our banner wave.
Be proud and thankful for their sacrifice,
Of which our fallen gave.

Funny Poems

SANTA'S PERSONAL AD

Exactly what would Santa do,
If he ever lost his wife.
Living with those little Elves,
Could be a lonely life.
Would he place a personal,
And look for love this way?
It makes you kind of wonder,
Just what his ad might say.

Hi, my name is Nicholas,
Folks think that I'm a saint
I am an older gentleman,
I'm jolly and so quaint.
I've traveled the world several times,
I like golf but tend to slice.
My favorite restaurant is Hooters,
The girls are naughty and really NICE!

They say that thin, is really in,
But fat is where it's at.
Red is my favorite color,
And I like to wear a hat.
My hair and beard are really white,
Both are soft as silk.
I always have a bedtime snack,
Of cookies and warm milk.
I live way north of Canada,

Where nothing is close or near.
I own a little company,
And work one day a year.
I really enjoy children,
I stay out all night long.
My favorite kind of music is,
A peppy Christmas song.

I am seeking someone special,
Who would like to tie the knot.
You must be like my cocoa,
VERY, VERY HOT!
You must be attractive and petite,
And know how to love your man.
With a really big firm bosom,
And a shapely little can.

Cooking skills would be a plus,
Because I love chocolate cake.
There's nothing like a woman,
Who can really SHAKEN BAKE!
If this ad has interest,
Well, than get in touch with me.
Then you can come on over,
And sit upon my knee!

nick@kringeL org

Dear Santa

Please, be ever so careful,
It's time for your yearly trip.
Use caution on icy roof tops,
I don't want you to slip.

Watch out in California,
There's road rage in LA.
Beware in all the major cities,
Drive by's happen everyday.

Look for car bombs along the way,
Do you use Firestones?
Please don't get the Bird-Flu.
Stay out of no-fly zones.

Watch the New York Police Department
If you reach for your I.D.
Do you random test the reindeer?
Stay out of Southeast D.C.

Boy, you have so much of stress
As you work the whole night through.
When you make it to my house,
I have cookies and milk for you.

Rudolph D.O.A.

Rudolph had a little to much egg nog,
Over spiked with Jack.
His senses became very dull,
And His eyes were out of whack.

He thought it ok, to fly away,
On that Christmas night
The other Reindeer allowed him to,
Even though Rudolph wasn't right.

Now, unlike the song, Rudolph's gone,
Friends helped him seal his fate.
Because they let Rudolph drink and drive,
NOW, IT'S MUCH TO LATE!

Friends don't let friends drive drunk!

DEADHEAD WITH A MEMORY

I used to have a memory,
Until the Grateful Dead came along.
Was it music or religion
That I heard in every song?
For thirty years all was peaceful.
The party lasted for that long.
I won't forget Garcia
Even though my memory's gone.

Each night and every city
There was a different show.
I always felt guite at home
With thousands of people I didn't know.
It was the world's largest drug store
With everything from pot to blow.
Deadheads are lost without the music.
We have no place to go.

My mind is playing seek and hide.
Everything still looks tie-dyed.
I think my brain is really fried,
But boy, it sure was fun.
My mind is always playing tricks on me.
It was probably all the L.S.D.
Is there a Deadhead with a Memory?
Well, try and find me one.
Good luck, there are none.

Jerry and Elvis are now together.
They're both flying U.F.O.'s.
The mind and the band are both long gone.
But that's how the story goes.
My brain is really southern fried
From the snorting and doing bones.
I really think that mama was right,
I should have listened to George Jones.

MOTHER DEAREST

Oh, Mother, dearest Mother,
How the years have flown.
You once said that you couldn't wait
Until I had children of my own.

You hoped that they'd become my likeness,
Then I would truly see.
Well, it's been an education,
Mom, thanks for not killing me!

BALD HEADED MEN

Endless time before the mirror,
Mesmerized by a stare.
Looking at a shiny head,
Once home to healthy hair.

Many questions do arise,
Why is baldness so unfair?
How can it grow in my nose and ears?
But it won't up there?

I feel like a giant pencil
With an eraser that is gone.
People say that bald is sexy,
Boy, they're completely wrong.

Shave the hair off of your dog,
Could you pet it still?
I'm so tired of looking in the mirror,
And seeing Dr. PhiL

God either has a sense of humor,
Making me bald as bald could be,
Or, I was made in His perfect image,
And He's as bald as me!

HOW I NEED YOU

As a baby needs tobacco,
Like a blind man needs a book,
As a drowning man needs water,
Like Chicago needs a crook.

As Bill Gates needing money,
To pay his rent when due.
Like a mosquito needs an airplane,
That's HOW I NEED YOU!!!!

BACK TO SCHOOL

It could not have come too soon.
I really need a rest
The kids have been home far too long,
I was getting really stressed.

Now, they're going back to school.
What a break for me!.
My nerves are shot, and I am frayed,
It's time for therapy!

Zoloft, Prozac or a Valium,
My mind is going numb.
Time for me to snuggle with
A bottle of Lithium.

This may sound a little course,
Maybe even cruel
But, Hallelujah Jesus,
The kids are going back to school!

Telemarketers

Hello, Hello, Hello.
I said into the phone.
There must be someone there,
But, there is no dial tone.

After a little hesitation,
Suddenly there's a voice.
Asking for donations,
Or phone carrier of choice.

NO, I don't want magazines,
My house windows are just FINE!
Why are you calling me so late?
Isn't it after nine?

I DON'T need a stupid burial plot,
Boy, you are a CREEP!
I don't even have a septic system,
I just want to go to sleep!

NO, I don't need time shares,
MY insurance is OKAY!
I wish that telemarketers,
Would just go away!!!!

NO, I don't know of anyone
Else that you could call.
WAIT, there is my mother-in-law,
I think she needs them all!

Hard Luck

If it were not for bad luck,
I would have no luck at all.
All because Cupid's wandering arrow
Took a sharp, misguided fall.

So I now live with this curse
Because of Cupid's aimless hand.
That is why I'm so in love with,
Someone that I can't stand!

HENPECKED HUSBANDS

One thousand men stood gathered,
Before St. Peter at the gate.
Awaiting further instructions,
In the process of their fate.

St. Peter then let out a yell,
"You men form a line of two."
"This will expedite the system,
"Of getting you guys through."

"Henpecked husbands while on Earth
Line up in this spot."
"The rest of you stand over there,
If henpecked husbands you were not"

The bewildered, henpecked husbands
Stood nine hundred and ninety nine.
But of the husbands never henpecked,
Only one stood in that line.

"Is this really where you should be?"
St. Peter asked the question clear.
The man replied, "OF COURSE NOT,
But my wife told me to stand here! "

MOTHER-IN-LAW

Honey, I have a problem
With what my mother just told me,
And it's upsetting me a little,
Because we disagree.

She wants to be cremated
And placed inside an urn.
Tell me how you feel about it.
I don't know which way to turn.

Wife, in fair and total honesty,
I see nothing wrong with that.
I'll even help with her request,
Tell her to grab her coat and hat!

Bedtime Prayer

Now it's time to close my eyes
So that I can get my rest,
Lord, if you take me on this night,
I have but one request.

Place a politician and a lawyer
On both sides of me please.
So I may die like Jesus did,
Surrounded by liars and thieves.

Lost Without You

You once told me that you loved me,
I know that's what I heard,
Softly spoken in clarity,
But you didn't keep your word.

I'll be such a mess without you,
Lost, with an unfound way.
Next time that you say I Love You,
Mean the words that you say.

I'm not bitter, nor am I angry,
My hearts door is opened wide.
When you figure your life out,
You'll be welcomed back inside.

I wish you all the luck,
And that you steer away from pain.
I hope that you find happiness,
For I only wish you gain.

I'll remember what you taught me
Before our time was through.
So none of this is the truth,
Because I'm lying just like you!!!

A Prince Amongst Toads

Is there a Prince amongst you,
to ease my many loads?
My lips are turning shades of green
kissing all these toads.

It's really nothing like the book
That I read when as a child.
Surely there's a Prince somewhere
Amongst these toads running wild.

So many men are out there
Of all kinds and different sorts.
With the way that things are going,
I'll get a case of warts.

Oh Prince, Oh Prince, where are you?
This is not a joke.
Every time that I kiss a man,
He begins to croak!!!!!!

Spiritual

JUDGING OTHERS

Sadly, we are always critiqued,
By the people that we know.
By title or occupation,
And by the possessions that we show.

We judge by skin color,
Or by awards received.
By church denomination
And by what we believe.

We're judged by what we spend,
Or by what we give.
We're judged by age and gender,
And by where we live.

We're judged by our past,
And by our education,
By the language that we speak,
Or by our nation.

We evaluate cosmetically.
We judge both fat and small.
We judge by ones appearance.
Fact is, we judge it all!

Some judge because they're paid to.
Some judge intentionally.
Some judge to build self worth,
Some judge unwillingly.

BEWARE, for there is only One,
Who evaluates every stain and smudge.
Good luck amateur critics of humanity,
When you face that Judge!

THE TOMB

In a cave so cold,
Wrapped in a garment of death.
After three days He arose,
With eternal breath.

A prophecy now fulfilled,
The stories soon began.
Of how Jesus truly was,
The Holy Son of Man.

Within your heart on this day,
Is there a place for Christ to room?
Will you choose the warmth of His love?
Or, the chill of the tomb?

THE TRENCHES

Life has changes along its way,
Similar to the weather it is day by day.
Be prepared come whatever may,
The skies turn quickly from blue to gray.

Sometime we are caught unaware
Easily dishearten when life's unfair.
No matter your burden, concern, or care,
You're never alone for someone's there.

Whether your problems are many or but a few,
There is Someone who will pull you through.
His promises made, are promises true.
God is in the trenches along with you.

THE PROMISE

The path is rough that you now walk,
Underneath a constant cloudy sky.
Lately, life has been so difficult
Some how you're getting by.
Remember a crop destroyed by Locust,
God promised to replace.
Keep your faith strong, firm and long,
On the problems that you now face.

Good Hands

Today, I asked almighty God,
In a very special prayer.
To touch you in this time of need,
And to feel His presence there.
God's promises spoken are promises kept,
His children, he never strands.
I just wanted you aware,
That, I left you in good hands.

THORNS OF MAN

We all have thorns, that we must bear.
It is a common thing all humans share.

So we ask the Lord, if He could remove
Those menacing thorns, to make life smooth.

There's a reason, they're allowed to penetrate
For it's our weaknesses, that makes Him great.

FEARS BONDAGE

Just a thought
That you need to host.
Never fear at all
What you fear the most.

Attack fears head on.
Do not avoid, nor swerve.
For it will only restrict
What you deserve.

The risk of hurt,
Is just a game of chance.
If you fear the music
You will never dance.

If failure has given you
Bitter taste and tears,
Remember, God loves your faith,
Satan loves your fears.

Encouragement

Problems sometimes shower us,
Where, we get caught up in the rain.
Overtaken by circumstances,
This may lead us to pain.

Then the storms end often seems,
Not within our sight
Will there be a dawn,
To end this darkness of the night?

One promise that you can focus on,
When your problems start to amass.
Remember Jesus Christ once said,
"So this too shall pass."

Payment Due

Is your life a living credit card?
Enjoy it now without sacrifice.
Don't even think about it
Why worry about the price?

Now it's a convenience,
There is no accountability.
I am doing something very nice.
I am really treating me.

Eventually you will max your limit,
An end comes to your spending spree.
Then the reality will set in
That nothing in life is free.

Everything comes at a cost,
Especially, living a wrongful way.
It may be fun for a while,
But someday you're going to pay.

Who Cares

Who cares if you're a Baptist,
Or a Catholic through and through?
Who cares if you're a Wesleyan?
Who cares if you're a Jew?

Who cares if you're a Pentecostal?
Who cares if you're Lutheran?
Who cares if you're a Methodist,
Or a Presbyterian?

Do you really think God cares about
The church that you call mine?
He gave all life and one book of rules,
That's His bottom line.

He cares that you hear and always practice
His written and spoken word.
Do you think that you're a Christian
When you don't practice what you've heard?

A church is not a temple
Where only the saints will show,
But rather, it's a hospital
Where only sinners go.

GARDENS

Our lives are similar to The Garden of Eden.
We have our own gardens in which we
should plant, maintain, and grow.
However, we spend more time trampling
down the flowers in other peoples gardens,
and forget about maintaining our own.
Because of neglect, our gardens then
become full of weeds and sin rules our lives.

FORGIVENESS

Jesus died upon the cross,
It was for gain, not for loss.
God sacrificed His only Son.
Forgiving us all for which we've done.

We are often hurt by others, too,
It's up to us on what we do.
Do not hang on, not one more day.
Let God take all your hurt away.

Don't be a bitter, but a better soul.
Resentment surely, will takes its' toll
Satan wants you hurting, for it is his way.
Free yourself from bondage today.

If you truly do want to live,
Think of someone that you must forgive.
A parent, spouse, child or friend,
Forgive them today, the pain will end.

Don't drag around a ball and chain.
Rid yourself of this needless pain.
To be like Christ, it must be done.
It is time for you to forgive someone?

THE PLUS

So your life is filled with negativity,
Everything is going wrong.
Most days you simply ask yourself,
"How can I carry on?"
Have you ever truly thought about
Letting Christ into your heart?
Give your problems to Him,
Today's the day to start.
Or, you could keep on ignoring Him,
And just complain and fuss.
But there is a special reason why
The cross is shaped just like a plus!

CROSSROADS

I come to You, oh Loving Lord
With decisions that I must make.
I am asking for a gentle push
Toward the path that I must take.

I know not where I goeth,
Keep me from going astray.
At the crossroads of this journey,
Guide me down the path You lay.

If I wander to the left
When I should have wandered right,
Keep those paths real close together
So that I may cross when back in sight.

Widen the path beneath my feet
So that I will not slip nor fall.
Walk me toward eternal life,
For I do not want to crawl.

I know You will not forsake me
As Your earthly children sometimes do.
Lead me down the path of righteousness,
For it will lead me straight to You.

Backsliding

Our Father, who art in Heaven,
Please listen to my prayer.
I'm Confused, frightened and alone,
But I know that You are there.

Lending an ear to all I ask for,
Lord, You determine my every need.
You are there when I am a failure,
And whenever I succeed.

I have been sliding backwards lately,
Now my life is in a spin.
Steady me and dust me off.
Place me on Your path again.

Never giving up on me,
You've been there each and every day.
Forgive me for my reckless actions,
Please turn me back Your way.

GOD'S LUMP OF COAL

Lord, I always wonder why
When bad things happen to me,
How could You allow me turmoil
And roughen waves upon my sea?

If you love me, why allow such pain
And unnecessary strife?
I thought thatYou wanted me to know
Peace within my life.

I know that You really love me,
I know that You really care.
I know that You work in mysterious ways,
I know that You are always mere.

"Child, you are pressed upon every side,
But you're never really broken.
I will keep My every word
On the promises that I've spoken."

"In time, I'll make it clear to you,
For now, your character I build anew.
I allow such problems to persist
So that you'll help others too."

"You are a special lump of coal,
There's a reason for the storms.
When coal is put under pressure,
Eventually, a diamond forms."

REJECTION

If God Himself is for you.
Then exactly who are they
That unleash their rejections
Casting you away?

Those of self condemnation?
Blind fools who cannot see?
Remember Christ too, was rejected,
So you're amongst great company!

GUARDIAN ANGEL

I need you, guardian angel,
To guard what I see and say.
Watch my every thought and move
Against whatever comes my way.

Temptation camps all around me.
More evil surfaces day by day.
Protect me from my oppressors
And all the traps they lay.

Keep me on the Fathers' path,
And do not let me stray.
Walk me through life's' many challenges,
Come whatever may.

The Reflection

You are His salt.
You are the light,
In a world uncertain,
In a world not right.

A representative of Jesus,
A reflection that people see.
Are you critical of others?
Or, do you act accordingly?

Will others see strength and joy?
Is there truth in what you teach?
Does your kindness infect others?
Do you practice what you preach?

We learn by simple example.
Do you set a good one, for all?
Are you a bridge to Jesus?
Or, are you a wall?

CAT OF NINE TAILS

A whip, with a distinctive sound,
When air whistles through the mesh,
Lashed across the Savior's skin,
Carving up His flesh.

Scourged not once, but thirty-nine times
Courtesy the cat tail strap.
Canals of blood lined his back
With every pain filled snap.

Through the streets Jesus dragged a cross,
Upon which His life would cease.
Crowds mocked, then spat upon,
This loving Man of Peace.

They bound His wrists to roughened wood,
Then placed a spike against His hand.
A hammer drove and sank it deep,
Blood squirting to the sand.

Two more spikes secured His body,
His cross was raised against the sky.
Completing a gruesome mission
Which was done for you and I.

HOMELESS

A homeless man or woman,
Another child of God.
You'll turn your back, and then walk away,
Because you find them odd.

No fireplace or warm, dry bed,
No family to call their own.
In the cold is where they sleep,
That's where they call home.

Exposed to natures elements,
On a frozen bench they lie.
While you sleep in your warm house,
Fed, secure, and dry.

That could have been you instead,
You are but one bad break away.
Then everyone can also treat you
Exactly the same way.

Buy them a warm and hardy meal,
And stop being critical.
Give them shoes without holes,
You can be the MIRACLE!

"Cast aside a brother, so too, shall I cast you."

Jesus Christ

TRIAL AND ERROR

My arms are stretched and opened wide.
Child, I've counted each tear you've cried.
Stubbornly, you seek resolution alone,
Your legs are long but you have not grown.

Withholding your problems so selfishly,
Refusing to pass them on to Me.
Fast to spin yet slow to gain,
Self progression dances with self pain.

Soon you will buckle from it all,
But I shall catch you as you fall.
Trial and error is how we learn
Next time you'll know which way to turn.

Rescue Me

Father I cry out to you,
It is dark and I cannot see.
Please, lead me through it all,
And I will go peacefully.
I thought that I knew everything,
Everything but you.
Just take away the darkness.
And let your light shine through.

I tried to do it on my own,
But I failed miserably.
Falling in between the cracks,
Will you rescue me?
No where to turn, no where but up,
Life is more than I can stand.
Lord, I now reach out to you,
Please take me by the hand.

Yes I turned my back on you,
To walk at my own pace.
I only saw life through my eyes,
Now I'm begging for your grace.
The easy steps became more difficult,
It's so hard to make it through.
Turn me back from my own path,
And lead me back to you.

GOD'S ANGEL'S

God has a mighty army
Of Angels everywhere.
Some you cannot see,
Others, our daily lives they share.

All have been summoned here
For specific reasons.
Some are here for an extended time,
Others for shorter seasons.

Angels guide, teach, and protect
Or shape our lives some way.
No one, only God Himself,
Knows why Angels cannot stay.

The Lord's ways are far too big
For us to fathom why,
But in time, we'll see in clarity
Why Angels say goodbye.

MISERY LOVES COMPANY

When Satan reminds you of the past,
And how you use to be.
Simply remind Him of the future,
And His Destiny.
Thought control is just a tactic,
To trip you foolishly.
Unlike Him, the slate can be cleaned,

MISERY LOVES COMPANY.

WHO AM I ?

I am the light after the rain,
I am the reliever of all pain.
I am all truth above a lie.
I am the shoulder on which you cry.

I am the ear that hears all prayers.
I am the keeper of all cares.
I am the eyes of all seen.
I am a body on which you lean.

I am the feet on which you land.
I am a rock for you to stand.
I am love and your best friend.
I am eternal without an end.

I am the door through all must pass.
I am a hand for you to grasp.
I am a compass if you lose your way.
I am a bridge with no toll to pay.

I am the link between Heaven and Earth.
I am the reason for your self worth.
I am forgiveness of all sin.
I am the race that you will win.

I am is my Father's name.
I am called the very same.
I am the precious Son of Man.
Jesus Christ is WHO I AM.

Unconditional Surrender

Oh, Prince of Peace,
Please grasp my hand.
I seek your help
In this unloving land.
Guide me, protect me
Only as You can.
Embrace me, secure me,
Oh, Holy Son of Man.

For I am a lamb
Which has strayed,
Embellished with pain,
Oh, the price I've paid.
Nurse me, heal me,
Build my life anew.
Lift me, nourish me,
As only You can do.

Oh, Jesus, sweet Jesus,
What salvation You do bring.
I surrender all to You today,
My great and glorious King.
Teach me, enlighten me,
For your wisdom I do yearn.
Forgive me, forgive me,
For being slow to learn.

BE STILL

Upon you I do wait, oh Lord,
For I need Thy guiding hand
Take me through this maze of confusion,
To rock not sinking sand.

You have seen the tears spill openly
And have heard my pleading prayer,
For in the valley of the shadows,
You were standing there.

Give me light, so that I may see,
To lead me along the way.
Hold my hand and lead me through
Yet , another cloudy day.

Tell me what You want of me.
I shall accept Thy will
I must be patient for You to act
While learning to be still

PATIENCE

Patience is a virtue,
As it shall always be.
Give time for it to happen.
Then you will truly see.

Just how perfect God's plans are,
For they are a masterpiece.
In time He'll expose it all to you,
Then those problems, they shall cease.

Your prayers turn into answers.
It may not happen overnight,
But you will get the gift as promised
When the time is right.

God stirs a lot of love
Into His special blend,
Then cooks it to perfection,
He's your Father and a Friend.

God takes care of His children.
Be patient, things will be just fine.
He'll take care of the neediest first,
So relax, you're probably next in line.

SATAN'S REMINDERS

Satan sends out reminders
Of how I used to be.
Doing it just to bring me down.
Instead, it adds strength to me.

I always tell Satan, "thank you ",
His reminders have me thrilled,
For my sins lie beneath the cross
Where Jesus' blood was spilled.

Jesus' mercy, love and grace,
Will always make me strong.
So Satan, go ahead, remind me of
All the things that I've done wrong.

Thank you, Lord, for hanging there,
Blood-soaked hands spiked to roughened wood,
When I'm reminded of my bad,
I will always see Your good.

So when Satan reminds you of your mistakes,
Remember your past, it has been waived
Through the precious blood of Jesus,
By His grace you have been saved.

Choose Your Words

Satan wants to test your strength,
He wants the chance to make you weak.
Protect what rolls from your lips,
Guard against the words you speak.

Satan cannot read your thoughts,
He goes by what you say.
Once he learns your weaknesses,
Then he will tempt you everyday.

So no matter who you are,
Choose your words with wit.
Everyone of us has weaknesses.
Be careful of what you admit

Tug Of War

Do you ever feel like you are caught in
A spiritual tug of war.
Where your soul is the battleground
And you can't take it anymore?

The closer that you get to God,
The more resistance you will meet,
God will try to stabilize your life.
Satan tries to knock you off your feet.

God wants you faithful.
Self-satisfaction is the devil's tool.
So the battle rages inside of you
On just who is going to rule.

The more Godly that you do become,
The more things will go wrong.
Satan is trying to make you weak,
God is trying to make you strong.

You contemplate giving in to evil
To end the struggle within you.
Our nature seeks the easy out,
Just what Satan wants for us to do.

Put on the armour of the Lord.
Soon Satan will turn and flee.
He will only win if you want him to.
Do not sell short of eternity.

The Eye Of God

He can see deep in my heart.
He can see my every tear.
He can see my every motive,
And my every fear.

He can see my every action.
He can see my every care.
He can see me when I'm selfish,
And each time that I share.

He can see my every struggle.
He can see when things are great.
He can see me when I love,
Also, when I hate.

He can see me when I'm strong.
He can see when I am weak.
He can see when I am honest,
And when I lie or sneak.

He can see my every thought.
He can see my every mood.
He can see when I'm compassionate,
And see me when I'm rude.

He can see me when I'm angry.
He can see when I am nice.
He can see me when I'm greedy,
And when I sacrifice.

His eye is always focused,
On all things that I do.
So when you think that no ones looking.
Remember, God is watching you!

THE BEACON

Standing proud, darkness around,
Salty air, the ocean sound.
Pounding waves rampage its base,
Planted firm in a strategic place.

Seen for miles, sending out a gleam.
A friendly beacon, a safety beam.
Its solid base will withstand a storm
Of any size or any form.

When the fog moves in and ships lose sight,
It will cast out a guiding light
Something that sailors will not ignore,
For it shall guide them safe to shore.

God is like a lighthouse, too.
For your own safety, He is there for you.
God's beacon is His guiding hand
Leading you to safe, dry land.

Stormy waters may toss you high and low,
God's beacon will lead you where you must go.
Just like a sailor, you need to trust.
God's light is faith, and it's a must.

LORD IM GOING TO TRY

Father please forgive me
For all my sins incurred,
For the countless times of negligence,
And failed practice of Your word.

Lord accept my somber apologies,
For I have brought You shame.
Forgive me for all that I have done,
And failed glory to Your name.

Oh, please wash and cleanse me,
Remove this soiled stain.
Through this sin filled life I have toiled
Self-inflicting needless pain.

I'm not worthy of Your glory,
Humbly, I seek Your grace.
Someday I will bow before You,
And confess all face to face.

This moment forth I pledge my best
Praying that I don't fall shy.
Although human, I'm prone to mistakes,
But Lord, I'm going to try.

The Eyes Of Jesus

Through the eyes of Jesus,
Blind as blind could be,
He did not notice size nor color,
Race or nationality.

He could not focus on your past,
Or, stature in society,
Your level of education,
Riches or poverty.

No matter who, what, or where,
He loves all equally.
If it was not for such loving blindness,
He would not have died for you and me.

SOMEWHERE

Somewhere we lost the meaning
Of how life's supposed to be.
Greed and selfishness are the cataracts
Which blinds us not to see.

The seven deadly sins prevail
In our suicidal society,
Engulfed in horrible bondage,
Unable to break free.

Destroying our own precious Earth,
The water, land and air.
Is anything really going to change
If we don't really care?

We are very self destructive,
Trapped within our deadly lair.
We have lost the meaning of it all,
Somewhere.

JUST ASK

When circumstances better you
Or, problems mount up everywhere.
if you are feeling overwhelmed
It is time to say a prayer.
Close your eyes and lift up your heart
God can handle any task.
If you need resolution,
All you have to do is ask!

PROBLEMS

Problems sometimes shower us,
And we get caught up in the rain.
Overtaken by circumstances,
Leading us to pain.
The storms end often seems,
Not within our sight.
Will there be a dawn,
To end this darkness of the night?
One promise that you can focus on,
As problems start to amass.
Remember Jesus Christ once said,
"So this too shall pass."

The Man From Galilee

Just as pure as pure could be,
Came a man from Galilee.
Words as plain as His cloak,
Captivating all ears to which He spoke.

His holy feet walked upon sinful sand
Clotting the wounds of a desensitized land.
Spreading the word which He was delivering,
Son of a carpenter, a Heavenly King.

Feeding all morsels from His righteous plate,
One course, sole purpose, solidified fate.
Betrayed by His own, a nation of fools.
Who chose to live life by their own set of rules.

Beaten, paraded, blood marking a course.
Crowds spat upon Him, without remorse.
Nailed to a cross for all to see
Hung the Man from Galilee.

BRIDGE OF LOVE

The distance between our Maker
And a sinful world grew.
Something had to happen
To close the gap between the two.

So God used a single cross
To build a bridge across this span,
Held together by nine inch nails
And one Son of Man.

He glazed it with painful tears
Along with the Saviors blood,
As Christ's life slowly trickled
Below into the mud.

Mostly women stood and watched
This man they so admired.
The bridge, became completed
When Jesus' breath expired.

God granted us forgiveness
For all that we had done.
He built a bridge of love
Using His only Son.

Starting Today

Lord, help me to know,
What needs to be known.
Teach me to see
What needs to be shown.

Please, touch my heart
As you always do.
Help me to exercise
What you ask me to.

Lord, take this cup
So that I don't spill
My problems no more,
For I want Thy will.

Oh, guide me, Father
Along Thy way,
I will give you my problems,
Starting today.

DEAR JESUS

Dear Jesus, it is only me,
One not worthy of your touch.
I have a request to ask of You,
Because you care for me so much.

There are problems in my life now,
That I need to give to you.
Please take them from these humble hands.
And help me work them through.

I live in a loveless world right now.
That's filled with hate and selfishness,
With people who have lost all faith,
Lord, things are such a mess.

I know that you truly understand
That my hands are tightly tied.
We have one thing in common, Lord,
We've both been crucified.

Your Father raised You from the cross,
When your life ended because of sin.
Resurrect me now, my Prince of Peace,
And let me live again.

Printed in the United States
89370LV00007B/217-225/A